ARSÈNE WENGER

HAIKU

俳句

BLINK

bringing you closer

Published by Blink Publishing

3.08, The Plaza,

535 Kings Road,

Chelsea Harbour,

London, SW10 0SZ

www.blinkpublishing.co.uk

facebook.com/blinkpublishing

twitter.com/blinkpublishing

Hardback – 978-1-7887-0135-8

Ebook – 978-1-7887-0136-5

A CIP catalogue of this book is available from the British Library.

Typeset by Envy Design

Printed and bound in Great Britain by Clays Ltd, Elcograf S.p.A.

1 3 5 7 9 10 8 6 4 2

Every reasonable effort has been made to trace copyright holders of material reproduced
in this book, but if any have been inadvertently overlooked the publishers would be glad
to hear from them.

Blink Publishing is an imprint of Bonnier Books UK

www.bonnierbooks.co.uk

Introduction

After 22 years and 1,235 games at the club, Arsène Wenger finally hung up his silly sleeping bag jacket in May 2018. Before he joined Arsenal in 1996, amid the bewildered cries of 'Arsène who?', he spent a year managing Nagoya Grampus Eight in the newly formed J-League in Japan. His tenure was a success, winning the Emperor's Cup and claiming the Coach of the Year award. Arsène's star was rising in the land of the rising sun and it did not take long for Europe to come calling again. Despite the sneers of Sir Alex Ferguson, who said: 'What does he know about English football, coming from Japan?', Arsène returned an inspired man: 'I learned there how to take hold of something by letting go... When I got back I was much more lucid, more detached, more serene.'

So as an 'Au revoir' to 'Le Professeur' and as a nod to his Eastern influences, here are 100 Japanese haiku – the famous 17- syllable poems – arranged over 3 lines – that chart his Arsenal career. They're formed from Arsène's famous quotes and quotes about him from rivals, critics and tributes from former players. Despite my resistance to positional changes, it should be pointed out that I have sometimes dispensed with the 5-7-5 formation to maintain the purity of my vision. And so, like the signing of Monsieur Vieira, I have added the odd syllable to strengthen the midfield. And like Monsieur Gallas, I have cast aside a troublesome syllable to tighten up the back line. And occasionally, like with Bendtner, I've forced something to work without rhyme or reason.

The book is split into four 'seasons', charting Arsène's time at Arsenal; the 'Spring' awakening (1996–2000), the heyday of 'Summer' (2001–2005), an 'Autumn' period of changes (2006–2010) and a barren 'Winter' with a couple of FA-cup shaped Christmas presents (2011–2018).

Merci Arsène!

SPRING

1996–2000

Tony Adams, then Arsenal captain, admitted asking himself this question when Arsène joined Arsenal on 22 September 1996.

Arsène Who?

A cautious welcome

What does he know about football?

Arsène who?, they asked.

Arsène's opening comments during his unveiling at Highbury on 22 September 1996.

A Message

First day at Highbury.
Come, watch us and be happy:
My message to fans.

Arsène's public message to Arsenal fans in September 1996 following news of his appointment as manager.

On Quality

Fame can be short term
The quality of your work
Survives the longest.

Arsène ended former manager Bruce Rioch's policy of allowing the players to eat chocolate before games, so a few disgruntled players began this cheeky chant from the back of the team bus on their way to Arsène's first away match. According to David Dein, Arsène turned round, wagged his finger and said 'Oh no.'

Team Bus

Boss bans chocolate!
'We want our Mars bars back',
The boys start to chant.

Arsène's reign begins at Ewood Park with a 2–0 win over Blackburn.

Beginnings

My first game begins,
Wright scores two at Ewood Park,
It starts with a win.

On 23 September 1996, in his first press conference as Arsenal boss, Arsène starts to win over the faithful with the perfect putdown.

Sleep

Late – in my hotel,
I tried to watch the Spurs match
But I fell asleep.

Arsène makes an accurate prophecy in late 1996.

A Prediction

Go forward ten years –
The best team in England will play
With seven or eight foreign players.

Captain Tony Adams admits to flouting the boss's strict diet by indulging in traditional Friday night fare in late 1996.

Captain Haddock

I looked at the Thames
Each Friday on Putney Bridge
With my cod and chips.

Arsène's team talks were famously silent for around ten minutes. He thought that players were in an 'emotional state' at half-time, so needed time to calm down.

A Team Talk

My half-time team talk:
(sound of wind blowing outside)
Silence is golden.

A slightly abbreviated version of Arsène's famous comment of 18 October 1996, having spent the previous year in Japan.

On Diet

I think in England

You eat too much sugar and meat

Not enough veggies!

Arsène highlights one of his guiding principles in October 1996.

The Light Within

I believe in humans
There's a light in everyone
That you can get out.

Arsène discussing the merits of striker Ian Wright on
24 November 1996.

One Strong Point

If you have one strong point
You are already lucky
Just play with it.

In his first full season, Arsenal won both the Premier League and the FA Cup – Arsenal's first domestic double since 1971; he also signed Emmanuel Petit and Marc Overmars, who became critical to Arsenal's success that year.

Double

My first full season
Overmars and Petit signed
We do the double.

Alex Ferguson responds, in April 1997, to Arsène's earlier claim that the fixture list was unfair and favoured Man United.

Opinions

He is a novice
He should keep his opinions
To Japanese football.

After Dennis Bergkamp performed yet another man-of-the-match display, Arsène offered a light-hearted response on 19 January 1997.

On Bergkamp

After every match
He gets a Champagne bottle
He can launch a shop.

Arsenal recorded ten successive victories between 11 March and 3 May 1998 to wrap up the title race with two games to spare.

Simplicity

Trailing by 12 points
Ten wins in a row
Man U overhauled.

Arsène opens up about what drives him before the FA Cup final on 16 May 1998.

Love to Win

You're a manager
Because you love to win
It lets you survive.

After the fans booed a stale 1-1 draw with Middlesbrough, Arsène muses on the rising expectations of supporters after the previous season's Double triumph.

Caviar and Sausages

If you eat caviar
Every day, it's hard to
Return to sausages.

*On 13 February 1999, a controversial winning goal
was set up by Nwankwo Kanu who had misunderstood
a situation when he should have followed sporting
convention and played the ball back to Sheffield United.
Arsène offered opposing manager Steve Bruce a replay.*

A Good Sport

We have the feeling

We didn't win like we wanted

I offered a replay.

Arsène in 1999 proving he's human, after all.

A Private Thought

Sometimes privately,
I say the referee was crap
But not publicly.

Arsène singles out his captain for praise in April 1999 while reminiscing about the outstanding defenders he inherited.

Dr Adams

A doctor of defence
He is simply outstanding:
Mr Arsenal.

Zlatan Ibrahimović recalls being asked by Arsène in 2000 if he would join Arsenal on trial. Suffice it to say Zlatan objected to the idea of auditioning.

Zlatan's Riposte

Ibra does not test
I will not do a trial
You take me or not.

In October 2000, Arsène was banned from the touchline for 12 games and fined £100,000 for allegedly shoving fourth official Paul Taylor after a match; he contested the charge, which was reduced to a reprimand, a £10,000 fine and a payment to cover the costs of convening the appeals board.

A Defence

I will first appeal
I may have to go to court
Unacceptable.

Arsène made this comment in December 2000 while Bergkamp was delaying signing a new contract; Bergkamp did sign it and stayed at the club for another six years.

A Pair

Kanu and Bergkamp
Together doesn't work
Not an ideal pair.

Arsène reiterates one of his core footballing beliefs before the away leg against Monaco in the Champions League Round of 16 in March 2015; Arsenal overturned a 3–1 loss at the Emirates with a 2–0 away victory, but they lost on away goals.

Belief

If you can't believe
Then you have no chance at all
You've already lost.

SUMMER

2001–2005

On 19 January 2001 Arsène makes his opinion clear on proposed EU reforms to players' contracts, which would allow them to move mid-contract.

Circus

It is not football
If they move every three months –
It is a circus.

Arsène outlining his measured approach to management on 23 November 2001, possibly compared to some of the other more irascible figures in the world of football management.

On Anger

If we lose a game
I don't kick doors, the cat, or
Even journalists.

Alex Ferguson voiced his disappointment on 10 March 2002 that Arsène was the only manager not to join him for a post-match tipple.

Snub

Never comes for a drink –
The only manager not to
It's a tradition.

Arsène revealing he's not omnipotent on 25 September 2002.

Deity

My powers have limits
I am not a witch doctor
I am just a coach.

A somewhat sarcastic Arsène in the wake of a 2–1 defeat at the hands of Borussia Dortmund in October 2002, following a controversial penalty; Arsenal still went through on aggregate.

Happiness

All credit to him,
The ref made a difference
I'm happy for him.

Arsène pondered this on 28 September 2002, just under a year before the start of the legendary Invincibles season of 2003–4.

A Frightening Thought

I am still hopeful.
A whole season unbeaten
A frightening thought.

No superlative can quite sum Henry up, but Arsène gave it a go on 14 December 2003.

Thierry

Thierry is amazing,
A dream you want as a player
We all play for him.

Alex Ferguson recalls the infamous match that ended Arsenal's historic 49-game unbeaten run. It was dubbed the 'Battle of the Buffet', on account of the foodstuffs that were launched in the tunnel after the game; one slice of pizza famously hit Ferguson in the face, which Cesc Fàbregas owned up to in 2017.

Pizza-face

Pizza all over me
Worst thing I've seen in this sport
They got off scot-free.

Arsène is livid at Man Utd striker Ruud Van Nistelrooy's conduct, specifically his studs-up challenge on Ashley Cole, during the 'Battle of the Buffet' match on 26 October 2004

Play Football,
My Friend

He can only cheat
People who don't know him well
Play football, my friend.

Taken from interviews with Arsène shortly after the legendary Invincibles season in 2004.

The Invincibles:
Jens Lehmann

Old Safe Hands retires,
Jens steps up between the sticks
Keeps 20 clean sheets.

Taken from interviews with Arsène shortly after the legendary Invincibles season in 2004.

The Invincibles: Sol Campbell

He came from the Lane
Such a power spread from him
A rock at the back.

Kolo Touré famously took out Henry, Bergkamp and Wenger with three terrible tackles during his trial in 2002; Touré thought he'd be fired but Arsène was really impressed with his commitment, saying: 'We're signing him tomorrow. I like his desire.'

The Invincibles: Kolo Touré

He takes out the boss
In his first training session
Tough-tackling Touré.

Ashley Cole was a product of the Arsenal youth system. According to Arsène, Cole left due to a misunderstanding between his agent and the club, which was something the Arsenal manager regretted.

The Invincibles:
Ashley Cole

Comes up through the ranks
One of the best in the world
He shouldn't have gone.

Taken from interviews with Arsène shortly after the legendary Invincibles season in 2004.

The Invincibles: Lauren

Mentally very strong
Cameroon's finest right back
A fantastic guy.

Patrick Vieira was actually signed before Arsène officially joined Arsenal, but it had been on Wenger's recommendation.

The Invincibles:
Patrick Vieira

Charisma, class, spirit,
The first player I brought here.
Legend, through and through.

Taken from interviews with Arsène shortly after the legendary Invincibles season in 2004.

The Invincibles:
Gilberto Silva

Shielding the defence
He sacrifices himself
A top-class person.

Taken from interviews with Arsène shortly after the legendary Invincibles season in 2004.

The Invincibles:
Robert Pirès

Cuts in from the wing
Armed with vision, flair and guile
Ahead of his time.

Taken from interviews with Arsène shortly after the legendary Invincibles season in 2004.

The Invincibles:
Freddie Ljungberg

A model professional
Scores on debut against Man U
The heart of a lion.

Taken from interviews with Arsène shortly after the legendary Invincibles season in 2004.

The Invincibles:
Dennis Bergkamp

Immaculate touch
The peerless perfectionist
A beautiful mind.

Taken from interviews with Arsène shortly after the legendary Invincibles season in 2004.

The Invincibles: Thierry Henry

He scores when he wants
Impossible to defend against
The greatest Gunner.

Arsène references Henry's goal via a quickly taken free kick on 18 January 2004 against Aston Villa, which the Villa players protested furiously.

On Fairness

It was a strange goal

He took a quick decision

Fair or not, I don't know

Arsène downplays the rumours in July 2004 that
Patrick Vieira wants to move to Real Madrid.

Vieira

I'm not in his head
It's the usual summer story
It's newspaper talk.

An extremely happy Arsène comments in August 2004 on Real Madrid's usually irresistible lure failing to work this time, as Vieira signs a contract to keep him at Arsenal until 2007; he left for Juventus in 2005.

Rebuffed

I am very pleased
They usually get what they want
This time it didn't work.

As a rematch with Man United followed on 31 January 2005, Arsène pointed out that Arsenal's 'dirty team' tag wasn't justified – they had gone a whole year without a red card.

Clean

Fewer fouls committed

Most sinned against? Who is it?

Arsenal FC.

After the 4–2 loss to Man Utd at Highbury on 31 January 2005, Arsène conceded the title to Chelsea.

Concession

It is Chelsea's now
There is too much for us to do
But we still have pride.

Arsène reacted angrily to an article in The Independent on Saturday on 18 January 2005 in which Alex Ferguson claimed Wenger owed him an apology for the 'Battle of the Buffet' match.

At His Feet

I don't understand
How he can do what he wants
And you're at his feet.

José Mourinho made these cutting remarks about Wenger on 31 October 2005 following Arsène's comments about Chelsea's recent performances.

Voyeur

He is a voyeur
Looking through a telescope
It is a sickness.

Arsène didn't hold back in November 2005 with his retort to Mourinho's 'voyeur' comment.

On Mourinho

He's out of order
Give success to stupid people
It makes them more stupid.

AUTUMN

2006–2010

Arsène addresses speculation that Real Madrid were trying to lure him away in April 2006. Later it transpired that Wenger did meet with Real Madrid presidential candidate Villar Mir and was offered a contract but Mir lost the election.

Arsènal

If I left the club
I'd feel like a deserter
I love what I do here.

Arsenal lost the 2006 Champions League final 2–1. Jens Lehmann was sent off in the 18th minute for bringing down Samuel Eto'o, but Arsenal went 1–0 up after 37 minutes courtesy of a Sol Campbell header. However, Henrik Larsson's introduction just after the hour mark swung the match, with Larsson setting up both Barca goals.

A Regret

Lehmann sent off
Sol gives us hope
But Barca too good.

Arsène famously likened national team coaches to 'joyriders' in October 2006 for the way they treat club players before returning them with various injuries.

Joyriders

First they take your car
Then leave it with no petrol.
Now it's broken down.

In May 2018, Arsène spoke emotionally about the special spirit of Highbury and how painful it was to move on 7 May 2006.

Goodbye, Highbury

It's a cathedral, a church.
It will always be special to me
Farewell to Highbury.

Arsène deftly responds to a complaint about the lack of English players at Arsenal by the Middlesbrough chairman in February 2007

A Maxim

My philosophy:
We do not buy superstars
We make them instead.

Arsène accused the assistant referee of the 2007 Carling Cup final of telling a 'lie' over the sending off of Emmanuel Adebayor; Wenger was fined. The 2006–7 season ended in disappointing fashion with only three wins out of the final ten Premier League games resulting in a fourth place finish (again) and a 2–1 Carling Cup final loss to Chelsea. But at least they finished above Tottenham…

Mind the Gap

Mon dieu! Fourth once more
Heartbreaking League Cup final
But finish above Spurs.

Arsène explaining his transfer policy and defending his close control of the club's purse strings, 1 September 2007.

On Money

I speak my own mind
I don't agree with the report
Because for me, he lies.

When faced with a complaint by the Middlesbrough chairman about the lack of English players in the Arsenal side, Arsène uses a vintage metaphor to explain that it's quality that counts, February 2007.

Sommelier

It's like a good wine
You see how it tastes first
Then ask where it's from.

Arsène defending William Gallas's sit-down protest after Arsenal concede a late penalty against Birmingham City, February 2008.

Gallas

He was frustrated
Sometimes you have to get
Your frustrations out.

Arsenal fan Piers Morgan speaks out in November 2008 after Arsenal lose their third game in four.

Morgan

I feel blind fury
We've become a laughing stock
And I blame Wenger.

William Gallas was stripped of the Arsenal captaincy in November 2008 following an unprecedented verbal attack on his teammates while on international duty in France.

Gallas No More

Enough is enough
Breaking ranks for the last time
Captain Gallas no more.

Arsène finally addresses his notorious 'I didn't see it' claims after controversial incidents in matches, August 2009.

Myopia

Sometimes I see it;
But I say that I didn't
To protect my team.

*In August 2009, referee Mike Dean sent Arsène to the
stands at Old Trafford for kicking a bottle of water in
frustration, after Robin van Persie's equaliser was ruled
out for offside. Wenger later received an apology from the
Professional Game Match Officials Board.*

Sent Off

Thirty seconds left
They told me go to the stand
For kicking a bottle.

In September 2009, Arsène accused ex-Arsenal and Man City striker Emmanuel Adebayor of deliberately stamping on Robin van Persie's head; Adebayor was later charged with violent conduct by the FA but given a lenient, suspended two-match ban due to provocation from the Arsenal fans.

What Would Jesus Do?

If you are stamped on,
You don't say thank you very much
Only Jesus did that.

Arsène made these comments in a 2009 joint interview with The Times and The Daily Mail when asked if he thought football was artistic.

Art pt. 1

Who are the best?
When I see Barcelona
To me it is art.

Arsène made this comment when asked if there was one existing rule he would change; this came off the back of Rory Delap's long throws which helped secure a 2–1 victory over Arsenal the previous season.

Progress

The rule I would change?

Play throw-ins by foot. Why not?

The game would be quicker.

Arsène draws on his artistic sensibilities again in March 2010 in an interview with The Independent.

Art pt. 2

Football is an art
Much like dancing is an art
Only when well done.

Stoke manager Tony Pulis highlighting his antipathy towards Arsène in October 2010 after a series of fiery encounters between the two sides.

Pulis

I have got nothing
Against foreign managers
Except Arsene Wenger.

An animated Arsène explains on 24 September 2011 that he shields his young team by taking the flak for poor performances himself. Arsenal were experiencing a very bad start to the season, sitting in 16th place in the table.

A Polar Bear

People criticise.
I'm supposed to take the bullets
Like a polar bear.

WINTER

2011-2018

Arsène responds to a question in June 2012 from an Italian journalist about whether Robin van Persie would make a move to Juventus.

A Bet

He'll stay at Arsenal
If he moves there, I'll buy you
A Caramello.

Arsène's priceless response in April 2013 when asked about Spurs going out of Europe to Basle.

Focus

Don't mind and don't care
I'm concerned with what we do
We focus on ourselves.

It turns out it's not all broccoli and Evian for Arsène, as
he answers questions during a question-and-answer live
on Twitter on 12 November 2013.

Broccoli and Evian

Yes I do like chips
But I try not to abuse it
I prepare like a player.

An exasperated Arsène addresses a press conference in February 2013 before a Champions League last-16 game against Bayern Munich; he's asked about Arsenal's recent FA Cup defeat to Blackburn.

The FA Cup

I've won it four times
Who's won the FA cup more?
Give me one name.

Arsenal win their first major trophy in nine years beating Hull 3–2 in the FA Cup final on 17 May 2014.

The Return of the King

Nine years in the cold
A brave fightback at Wembley
Silverware returns.

Arsène becomes introspective after being presented with a golden cannon to mark his 1,000th game in charge of Arsenal on 31 March 2014.

A Scar

I'm a bad loser
Every defeat is a scar
You never forget.

Arsène jokes with the press in December 2014 explaining that there's a big difference between perception and reality.

A Date

You will understand
I'm not scared to spend money
If you go out with me!

Arsenal blow away Aston Villa 4–0 to retain the FA Cup on 30 May 2015, with Santi Cazorla winning the man-of-the-match award.

'Santa' Cazorla

Christmas comes early
Arsenal cruise to the cup
With Santi the star.

Arsène gets philosophical in a November 2015 interview with L'Equipe.

An Impossible Job

What you want changes
As soon as you have it
You always want better.

Arsène uses a delicate metaphor to explain the fragility of team spirit in October 2015.

On Botany

It's like a flower
You have to take care of it
Or else it will die.

Comments made in a November 2015 interview with L'Equipe.

On Teamwork

There is a magic
When men unite to express
A common idea.

Comments made in a November 2015 interview with L'Equipe.

Enlightenment

I'm only a guide
Allow others to express
What they have in them.

Comments made in a November 2015 interview with L'Equipe.

The Present

The past gives regrets
And future uncertainties
Happiness is now.

A witty yet combative response from Arsène to a question on Tottenham's rise in the 2015–16 season; Arsenal finished one point above Spurs – the 21st consecutive season they had finished above their North London rivals.

Mind the Gap pt. 2

Have Spurs closed the gap?
They're still four miles and
11 titles away.

An irate Arsène decries two dubious decisions that allowed Man City to come from behind and beat Arsenal 2–1 at the Etihad in December 2016.

Caged Animals

We are used to it
Referees are protected
Like lions in the zoo.

Arsène thinks back, in December 2017, to his first season at Arsenal and how he couldn't have predicted that he'd still be in charge 21 years later.

I'm Still Standing

It's Russian roulette.

Every game is a gamble

But I'm still standing.

Arsène muses on the nature of confidence after their second 3–0 defeat to Man City in the space of a week, in March 2018.

What is Confidence?

You go up the stairs
And you come down by the lift
That is confidence.

Arsène deflects attention away from his team with a typically abstract comment following defeat to Brighton in March 2018.

Naked

When you are naked
You have to find a shirt, then
Put it on again.

Comments made in a November 2015 interview with L'Equipe.

On Work

I'm not on Twitter
I work and work and work
That's all I can do.

Arsenal legend David Seaman calls on anti-Wenger supporters in April 2018 to get out and support him following the news of Arsène's imminent departure at the end of the season.

Respect

Get behind Arsène

Give him the respect he deserves.

It's time to show respect.

Former captain Cesc Fàbregas on Twitter, 20 April 2018.

Father Figure

He had faith in me
He was a father figure
I owe him a lot.

*Last man in, Pierre-Emerick Aubameyang on Twitter,
20 April 2018.*

The Final Signing

I'm your last signing
I'm proud to be your player
Thanks for everything.

Former captain Robin van Persie on Twitter, 20 April 2018.

Forever Thankful

I'll always see you
As my footballing father
Forever thankful.

Tony Adams offers his tribute to Arsène on Twitter on 20 April 2018; 'Herbert' refers to revered Arsenal manager Herbert Chapman (1925–1934).

Move Over Herbert

Thanks for everything.

Greatest Arsenal manager

Move over Herbert.

Arsène looks ahead to the future, May 2018.

In Red and White

I'll buy a ticket
Watch the games in red and white
And hope Arsenal win.

Part of Arsène's farewell speech to the fans at the Emirates on 6 May 2018.

A Way of Life

I'm an Arsenal fan
This is more than just football
It's a way of life.